**Jesus said,
"Love one another."**

John 15:12, adapted

FAITH WORD:
Cross

Love One Another

TODDLERS & TWOS – BIBLE STORY PICTURE CARDS / SPRING/ © 2004

MAIN IDEA:
Jesus wants us to love one another.

SHARING FAITH WITH YOUR CHILD
Toddlers and twos are just beginning to incorporate words with their strong feelings. It is their nature to strike out rather than to speak out when annoyed or frustrated. Patiently remind your child to use words when he or she is ready to strike out with teeth or hands. During play times together, create opportunities to use words during frustrating circumstances. Building a block tower that suddenly topples may inspire you to say, "Oh, no! My tower fell. I don't like that!"

When your child does lash out physically, be calm but firm. "No, biting hurts!" Show anger at your child's action, not at your child. Make sure he or she understands that violence is not allowed.

Pray: Thank you, God, for people to love.

March-April #1

Josh and Anna

"No! Go away, Anna!" grumbles Josh.

"Come play with me, Anna," calls Jesus. Anna happily goes to Jesus. "Josh, you come, too," says Jesus.

"Josh," Jesus says softly, "God loves little children. God loves little Anna. Be kind and show God's love."

"Anna, I'm sorry I was not kind," says Josh. Anna hugs Josh. Josh and Anna are happy.

"Thank you, Jesus, for teaching me how to show God's love," says Josh.

FAITH WORD: Cross

Jesus said, "Love one another."

John 15:12, adapted

Love One Another

TODDLERS & TWOS – BIBLE STORY PICTURE CARDS / SPRING/ © 2004

MAIN IDEA:

Jesus wants us to love one another.

SHARING FAITH WITH YOUR CHILD

When young children hear words to describe sharing, they acquire a greater acceptance of how to share. When your child is in childcare, there will most likely be several of each popular toy for children to use. As a grownup, it is important to remember sharing is not sacrifice. Applaud every effort your child makes to share with others. When two children are ready for the same toy, try to create play with both children and the toy. Shift the importance to the fun together.

Share the story on this card together. Eat a snack together as you look at the picture on the story card. Talk about the sisters who share bread and love together.

Pray: Thank you, God, for friends who share.

March-April #2

Sister Cares for Seta

"Hungry!" wails Seta. "I'm hungry!"

"Sit with me, Seta," says her big sister. "Sit with me and I will share bread with you."

Seta climbs into her sister's lap. Sister shares the bread with Seta. "Yum! The bread is good!" Seta says.

Seta hugs her sister. "Thank you," she whispers.

Sister remembers Jesus saying, "Show love to one another."

Love One Another

TODDLERS & TWOS – BIBLE STORY PICTURE CARDS / SPRING/ © 2004

MAIN IDEA:
Jesus wants us to love one another.

SHARING FAITH WITH YOUR CHILD
Parents often need to pass on information about their child's health or other matters to Sunday school teachers. When several parents and toddlers are added to the mix at drop-off time, actual communication may be elusive. Before leaving for church, write down any information you need to give the teachers. Being ready for a smooth transition adds to the comfortable feeling of routine for your child and other class members. Teachers will appreciate your thoughtfulness as well.

Share the story on this card with your child. Talk about how your child is learning about Jesus at church, just as Seth and Hannah listened to Jesus in the Temple. Help your child realize that we are still learning the same lesson every week: to love one another.

Pray: Dear God, help us to love one another.

March-April #3

Learning From Jesus

"Jesus is teaching at the Temple, Seth. I heard Jesus today," says Hannah.

"I like to hear Jesus, too, Hannah," Seth says. "Jesus says to love one another."

"I am happy to learn from Jesus," says Hannah.

**Jesus said,
"Love one another."**

John 15:12, adapted

FAITH
WORD:
Easter

Love One Another

TODDLERS & TWOS – BIBLE STORY PICTURE CARDS / SPRING/ © 2004

MAIN IDEA:
Jesus wants us to love one another.

SHARING FAITH WITH YOUR CHILD
Sharing faith does not mean "sit down and listen." Take a cue from the Bible story card this week and share faith with your toddler actively. Create an active story with a stuffed animal or doll. You and your toddler could take the doll for a walk by each holding a hand. Make rest stops to care for each other, with imaginary drinks of water, bandages for imaginary hurts, and so on. Use words to connect showing kindness and loving each other.

Use a familiar children's melody (such as "Twinkle, Twinkle, Little Star") to create together a song about showing love to others.

Say: I'm glad God gives us friends who show love.

Pray: Teach us, dear God, to love one another.

March-
April
#4

David Cares for Hannah

Run! Jump! Run! Jump! Hannah and David play in the sunshine.

Run! Jump! Run! Bump! Ouch! Hannah bumps her toe.

Run! Jump! Run! Stop! David waits and cares for Hannah.

Jesus says, "Love one another!"

Sing for joy to the LORD.

Psalm 98:4,
Good News Bible

FAITH
WORD:
Easter

Happy Easter!

TODDLERS & TWOS – BIBLE STORY PICTURE CARDS / SPRING/ © 2004

MAIN IDEA:
Easter is a happy time.

SHARING FAITH WITH YOUR CHILD
Have you ever heard a frustrated parent say something like, "I said stop that!" or "Don't do that again!"? For young children (and some not so young), these words hold little or no meaning. Give your child clear directions that are within his or her ability to understand. "Put the ball down, please" or "Do not hit" hold meaning a two- or three-year-old can grasp. Then your child can make a choice to obey.

Share the story on this card together. If appropriate, decide on some friends that your child may invite to accompany him or her to church.

Say: We are so happy about Easter that we want everyone to know.

Pray: Thank you, God, that Easter is a happy time!

March-April #5

John Goes to Church

"Where are you going, John?" calls Matthew.

"I'm going to church," John says with a smile at his friend. "I will listen to Jesus teach about God's love. Come with me."

"I will come with you, John," says Matthew. "I want to hear Jesus, too!"

Easter is a happy time!

**Sing
for joy
to the
LORD.**

Psalm 98:4,
Good News
Bible

FAITH
WORD:
Easter

Happy Easter!

TODDLERS & TWOS – BIBLE STORY PICTURE CARDS / SPRING/ © 2004

MAIN IDEA:
Easter is a happy time.

SHARING FAITH WITH YOUR CHILD
Repetition is important to how a young child learns. Adding to established skills and knowledge is an important key to all learning. Educators sometimes call this "activating prior knowledge." For you, as a parent, it means returning to the familiar and the routine your child enjoys. Your child gains understanding when you repeat important lessons.

Share the story on this card with your child. Name some of the children in your child's Sunday school class. If you have a photo of your child's Sunday school class, use it to point to the children as you talk together. Make it a point to invite friends of your child to learn about Jesus at church.

Pray: Thank you, God, for Easter.

March-April #6

Jesus Is Coming!

Leah runs to her friend and says, "Hurry, Anna! Jesus is coming!"

"Jesus is coming to Jerusalem?" asks Anna. "When, Leah?"

"Now! Come with me to welcome Jesus," says Leah.

"Yes, Leah," answers Anna, "I am happy to welcome Jesus!"

Easter is a happy time!

Palm Sunday

TODDLERS & TWOS – BIBLE STORY PICTURE CARDS / SPRING/ © 2004

MAIN IDEA:
We can praise God for Jesus.

SHARING FAITH WITH YOUR CHILD
Easter is a happy time. For our toddlers and twos, the excitement of Palm Sunday, with waving palm branches and calls of "hosanna," is clearly a happy time. Twos have no concept of death or betrayal. For our young children, it is enough to take part in the Easter story through celebrating the good news. Check the bulletin boards and newsletters and ask your child's Sunday school teacher for fingerplays and songs they will be using to celebrate Easter in class. Add them to your Bible story times at home.

Read the Bible story on this card to your child. Act out the story together using large movements to clip, clop like the donkey and waving your arms when calling "hosanna."

Palm Sunday

Pray: Thank you, God, for happy times at church.

Hosanna!

Jesus will ride a donkey to Jerusalem. Jesus will go to the Temple to teach the people about God. Jesus will help the people.

Clip, clop, clip, clop sound the donkey's feet.

"Hosanna, hosanna, hosanna!" shout the happy people.

Easter is a happy time!

Easter Sunday

TODDLERS & TWOS – BIBLE STORY PICTURE CARDS / SPRING/ © 2004

MAIN IDEA:
Easter is a happy time.

SHARING FAITH WITH YOUR CHILD
Young children learn to speak by hearing others speak. Lean down to your child's eye level when talking together. Say your words clearly, repeating any words your child may be working to understand. Older twos are ready to abandon baby talk as they opt for clearer and more complicated communication. Model clear speech and avoid too many pronouns. Provide names for objects beyond "thing," "it," or "stuff."

Toddlers and twos cannot yet understand the concepts around the death and resurrection of Jesus. Nevertheless, help your child experience the sadness and the joy of Easter with the story on this card. Help your child realize that Jesus' friends were happy to find him on Easter morning.

Easter Sunday

Pray: Thank you, God, for the happy times of Easter!

Happy Easter!

Mary cannot find Jesus. Mary feels sad, so sad. Mary starts to cry.

"Mary," calls a man, "why are you crying?"

"I came to find Jesus," cries Mary, "but he is not here."

"Here I am, Mary," says the man. Mary looks at the man. It is Jesus!

Jesus found Mary! Now Mary is very happy!

Easter is a happy time!

Teach Us to Pray

MAIN IDEA:
I can pray to God, just as Jesus did.

SHARING FAITH WITH YOUR CHILD
Toddlers and twos take time to examine and look closely at the wonders around them. Their wonder and exploration give the adults in their lives numerous opportunities to say prayers of thanks with them. Your child holds a stone up for you to see. You respond, "Oh, a stone. Thank you, God, for smooth, round stones. Thank you, God, for strong arms to pick up stones!"

Bring a paper plate and a spoon to Bible story time. Play "pretend meal" together. Begin by saying a prayer of thanks. Pass imaginary food to the plate and "eat" with the spoon. Don't forget to clean up!

Say: Jesus prayed when he ate food. We can pray, too.

Pray: Thank you, God, for our good food.

First Sunday of May

Jesus Prays

Many people listen to Jesus talk about God's love. Now the people are hungry.

"God gives us food to eat," Jesus tells the people. "Sit down."

Jesus prays, "Thank you, God, for good food to eat." He says, "We will eat now."

The people remember to thank God for good food, just as Jesus does.

Jesus said to always pray.

Luke 18:1, adapted

FAITH WORD: **Prayer**

Teach Us to Pray

MAIN IDEA:

I can pray to God, just as Jesus did.

SHARING FAITH WITH YOUR CHILD

Parents often find evening prayers with children are a meaningful part of a nighttime routine. Don't be surprised if along with a request for another drink, your child begins to ask for bedtime prayers. Take this quiet time to reflect with your child. This time will bring you unforgettable memories.

Evening prayers can become a list of "God bless (insert name)." Older twos may be receptive to sitting quietly with parents ("Be still, and know that I am God!") after being tucked in for the night.

Along with formal evening prayers and food time prayers, add spontaneous "Thank you, God" prayers to model praying all the time.

Second Sunday of May

Pray: Thank you, God, for all your care.

Pray All the Time

Jesus tells all the people that God loves them.

Jesus loves God. He talks to God every day. Talking to God is called praying.

Jesus tells all the people to pray.

He says to pray all the time.

FAITH WORD:
Prayer

Jesus said to always pray.
Luke 18:1, adapted

Teach Us to Pray

TODDLERS & TWOS – BIBLE STORY PICTURE CARDS / SPRING/ © 2004

MAIN IDEA:
I can pray to God, just as Jesus did.

SHARING FAITH WITH YOUR CHILD
Are you parenting an on-the-go two? Make an active prayer time. Lift your arms to show praise, hug yourself to express love, hop to show appreciation of all good things.

With your child, use the following active prayer:

Pray: God, you are good. *(Raise arms over head.)* Thank you for my mommy and daddy. *(Hug yourself.)*

Thank you for toys *(hop)* and pets *(hop)* and good food *(hop)*. Amen. *(Add to and change the prayer as you and your family choose.)*

Write words to your family's active prayer on a large piece of paper and use it during the week.

Pray: Thank you, God, for hearing our prayers.

Third Sunday of May

Jesus Prays

Jesus tells the people that God loves them. The people listen to Jesus.

Jesus says to pray. But the people say, "We don't know how to pray."

So Jesus tells them how to pray. He says, "When you pray, say, 'Dear God, you are great. Thank you for loving me. Amen.'"

Jesus said to always pray.

Luke 18:1, adapted

Teach Us to Pray

TODDLERS & TWOS – BIBLE STORY PICTURE CARDS / SPRING / © 2004

MAIN IDEA:
I can pray to God, just as Jesus did.

SHARING FAITH WITH YOUR CHILD
Take time to yourself to think about the meaning of prayer in your life. It may be helpful to write down your thoughts and to look over them in a few weeks. Consider the people you want to pray for you as you parent your child. Take a deep breath and know that God is with you; you are not alone.

One of the earliest prayers we teach our children is "God bless _____." While we often talk about this prayer with amusement, remember that this is an important step in learning about intercessory prayer. Help your child pray for others each night as you approach bedtime. Especially remember to celebrate with your child answered prayers.

Pray: Thank you, God, for hearing our prayers. Help us remember to pray for others. Amen.

Fourth Sunday of May

God Hears You

Jesus tells the people, "God hears you when you pray. You are God's children. God loves you very much."

"Where can I pray?" asks Susanna.

"God hears you even when you hide in a closet," says Jesus. "God hears you wherever you are."

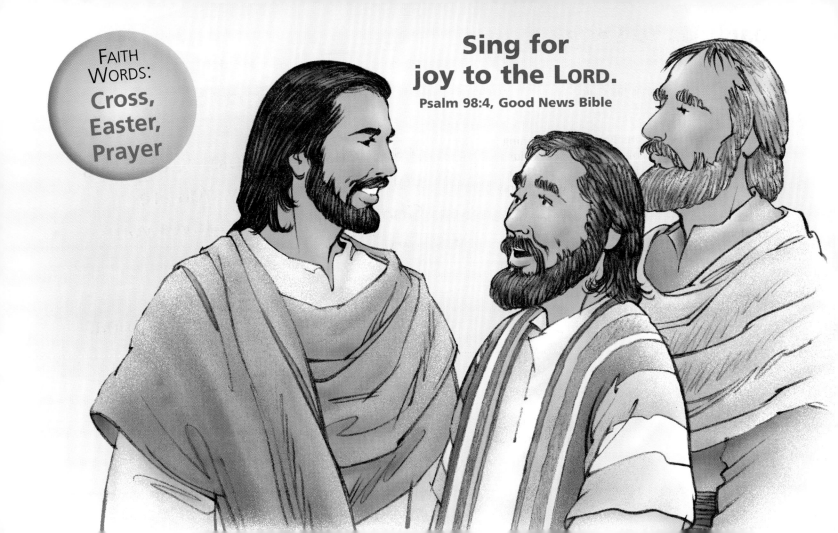

FAITH WORDS:
Cross,
Easter,
Prayer

Sing for
joy to the LORD.

Psalm 98:4, Good News Bible

Jesus Loves Me

TODDLERS & TWOS – BIBLE STORY PICTURE CARDS / SPRING/ © 2004

MAIN IDEA:
Jesus loves me just the way I am.

SHARING FAITH WITH YOUR CHILD
Young children can hear that God loves them, but to a toddler, God is a totally abstract concept that has no real meaning. Young children experience God's love through God's representatives—their parents and the adults whom they encounter in God's house. In other words, *you* represent God to your child.

Children who feel loved and accepted by adults when they are young have an easy time believing that God loves them when they are older. Children who do not learn to trust adults when they are young have a difficult time trusting in God when they reach adolescence and adulthood. The absolute best thing you can do to nurture your children's faith is to simply love them as they are.

Spring
Fifth
Sunday

Pray: Dear God, thank you for loving us. Amen.

Pray All the Time

James and Peter come to Jesus and say, "Sometimes we do not want to pray. Sometimes we think God does not love us anymore. We don't know when to pray."

Jesus says, "God always loves you, even when you don't think you are good enough. You should pray all the time. God will always love you and is always listening whenever you pray."

CHILD INFORMATION SHEET

Today's date: _____

Full name of child: _____

Name child is called: _____

Date of birth: _____

Is child baptized? _____Yes _____ No

Address: _____

Home phone: _____

Mother's name: _____

Address: _____

Home phone: _____

Work phone: _____

Cell phone: _____

E-mail: _____

Father's name: _____

Address: _____

Home phone: _____

Work phone: _____

Cell phone: _____

E-mail: _____

Who lives in the home with the child?
    (Name, relationship to child, age)

_____

_____

_____

Has the child been in group care before?

_____Yes _____ No

If yes, where? _____

_____

Was this group care a positive experience?

_____ Yes _____ No

Explain: _____

_____

_____

Does the child take regular naps?
If yes, what are his or her regular nap times?

_____

Does the child have allergies?

_____

_____

Is the child on any kind of regular medication?

_____ Yes _____ No   If yes, describe:

_____

_____

Is your child toilet trained? _____ Yes _____ No

What are the words your child uses for toileting?

_____

Describe some of the activities your child enjoys:

_____

_____

_____

What words would you use to describe your child?

_____

_____

Is there anything else your child's teachers need to know to best meet the needs of your child?

_____

_____

_____

_____